How Did They *Do That!*

Charles Hirsch and Susan Meyers

Contents

1 The World of Special Effects

Imagine yourself sitting in a dark movie theater. On the screen, a car is driving through a raging storm while trees fall around it and lightning flashes across the sky. Suddenly an enormous creature with razor-sharp teeth thunders onto the screen: Tyrannosaurus Rex! You almost drop your popcorn as the dinosaur rips through the roof of the car. You catch your breath as the car tumbles from the road and explodes in flames!

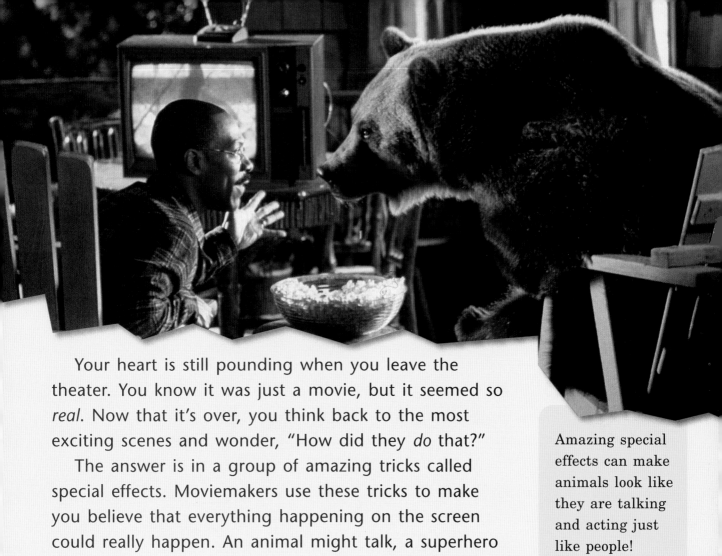

Your heart is still pounding when you leave the theater. You know it was just a movie, but it seemed so *real*. Now that it's over, you think back to the most exciting scenes and wonder, "How did they *do* that?"

The answer is in a group of amazing tricks called special effects. Moviemakers use these tricks to make you believe that everything happening on the screen could really happen. An animal might talk, a superhero might fly, or Earth might be invaded by enemy aliens.

Amazing special effects can make animals look like they are talking and acting just like people!

3

Water from a hose can make this car look like it is driving in a rain storm.

Special effects can be as simple as spraying water from a hose to create the appearance of rain or as difficult as building an army of computer-controlled spaceships. All kinds of artists, engineers, and craftspeople work with special effects. Model makers build tiny scale models, accurate to the finest detail. Robotics experts construct lifelike, remote-controlled animals. Computer programmers create amazing creatures and settings.

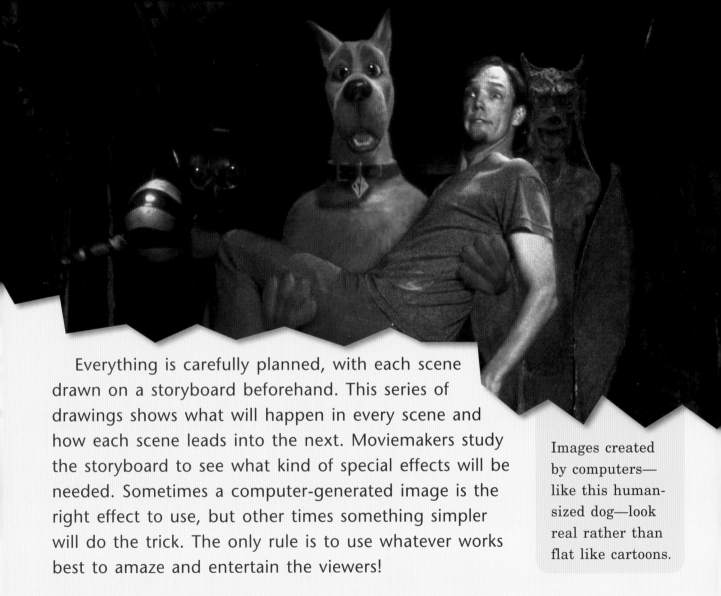

Everything is carefully planned, with each scene drawn on a storyboard beforehand. This series of drawings shows what will happen in every scene and how each scene leads into the next. Moviemakers study the storyboard to see what kind of special effects will be needed. Sometimes a computer-generated image is the right effect to use, but other times something simpler will do the trick. The only rule is to use whatever works best to amaze and entertain the viewers!

Images created by computers—like this human-sized dog—look real rather than flat like cartoons.

2 Make It Tiny. . . . Make It Huge!

If you visited a special effects workshop, you would probably see model makers constructing cars, planes, and spaceships so tiny that they could fit in the palm of your hand. You might also see pencils or blades of grass so large that they tower over a full-grown person. These are all scale models, one of the most important kinds of special effects used in movies.

Scale models are copies made to look exactly the same as the real thing, only much smaller or larger. Sometimes scale models are used because filming the real thing would be difficult, impossible, or simply too expensive.

This lizard-like creature destroying London is actually an actor in a costume stomping through a very small version of the city.

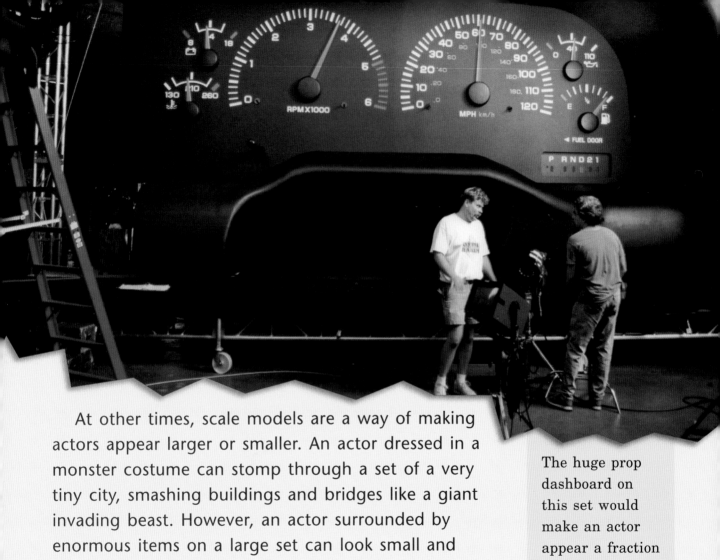

At other times, scale models are a way of making actors appear larger or smaller. An actor dressed in a monster costume can stomp through a set of a very tiny city, smashing buildings and bridges like a giant invading beast. However, an actor surrounded by enormous items on a large set can look small and threatened in a world of giant structures.

The huge prop dashboard on this set would make an actor appear a fraction of his true size.

7

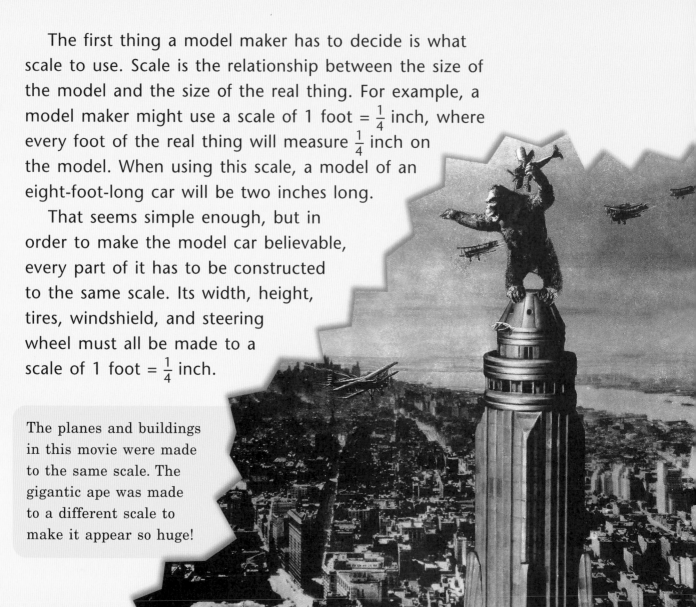

The first thing a model maker has to decide is what scale to use. Scale is the relationship between the size of the model and the size of the real thing. For example, a model maker might use a scale of 1 foot = $\frac{1}{4}$ inch, where every foot of the real thing will measure $\frac{1}{4}$ inch on the model. When using this scale, a model of an eight-foot-long car will be two inches long.

That seems simple enough, but in order to make the model car believable, every part of it has to be constructed to the same scale. Its width, height, tires, windshield, and steering wheel must all be made to a scale of 1 foot = $\frac{1}{4}$ inch.

The planes and buildings in this movie were made to the same scale. The gigantic ape was made to a different scale to make it appear so huge!

Everything in the scene with the model, such as buildings and trees, must be built to the same scale. Otherwise the car will look too big or too small and seem fake. This is a lot to remember, so model makers often use lists and charts that they refer to as they work.

Suppose the model maker wanted to use this scale to build a model of the Statue of Liberty, which is about 152 feet tall. How tall would the scale model be?

Scale:
1 foot = $\frac{1}{4}$ inch

Calculating Scales

Actual Size	Calculation of Scale	Scale Model Size
Car = 8 ft long	$8 \times \frac{1}{4}$ in = 2 in	Scale model of car = 2 in long
Bus = 36 ft long	$36 \times \frac{1}{4}$ in = 9 in	Scale model of bus = 9 in long
House = 20 ft tall	$20 \times \frac{1}{4}$ in = 5 in	Scale model of house = 5 in tall
Tree = 28 ft tall	$28 \times \frac{1}{4}$ in = 7 in	Scale model of tree = 7 in tall

Answer: 38 inches

9

3 Moving Step by Step

Once the scale models are built, moviemakers must film them to capture the special effect needed for the movie. If the scale model is just a background for an actor, it is easy enough for the camera to film the actor moving around. But what if the subject of the special effect *is* the scale model object itself, not an actor?

The moviemakers had to pose this model 24 different times to record 1 second of movement. Every detail of this 4-foot-high model must be perfect because when it is on the screen, it will appear many times its size.

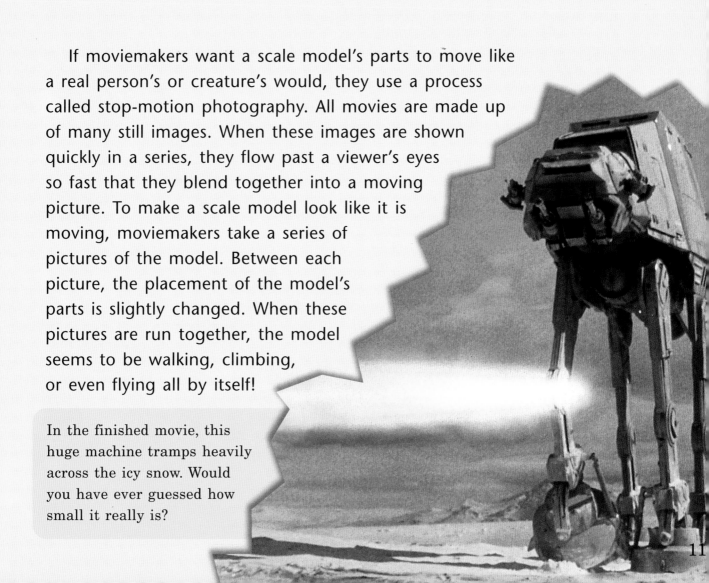

If moviemakers want a scale model's parts to move like a real person's or creature's would, they use a process called stop-motion photography. All movies are made up of many still images. When these images are shown quickly in a series, they flow past a viewer's eyes so fast that they blend together into a moving picture. To make a scale model look like it is moving, moviemakers take a series of pictures of the model. Between each picture, the placement of the model's parts is slightly changed. When these pictures are run together, the model seems to be walking, climbing, or even flying all by itself!

In the finished movie, this huge machine tramps heavily across the icy snow. Would you have ever guessed how small it really is?

11

Now these astonishing moving models can have adventures in their own small settings. It could cost thousands—even millions—of dollars to build a life-sized background for a dinosaur or an unusual alien. With scale models, moviemakers can create an entire world on an area no larger than a tabletop!

In some cases, moviemakers build part of a model that is almost as big as the object would be in real life *and* a complete, small model. This way they can get every shot they need, especially if real-life actors are involved.

This model is a scale version of a spacecraft. It is being prepared for a special-effects shoot which will make it appear to be life-sized on camera.

Actors perform their parts on the large model, which is only a small part of the boat or spaceship in the movie. The moviemakers film the large object so that we see only part of it and don't notice that anything is missing. Then they film the smaller model sinking at sea or zooming through space and landing on a distant planet. When they put both shots together, it looks like the actors really were on a huge boat or a giant spacecraft.

This spacecraft model is as big as a real spacecraft!

13

4 Strange Beasts

What is another way to create a dinosaur, a dragon, or an alien from a distant planet that looks completely real on the screen? A process called animatronics is sometimes used to bring full-sized models of animals and imaginary creatures to life. It begins with a plastic animal fitted over a frame made of parts that can be moved by remote control. Hair, skin, and teeth are added to make the creature look as real as possible.

Would you believe that this dog and this cat are animatronic creatures, not real animals?

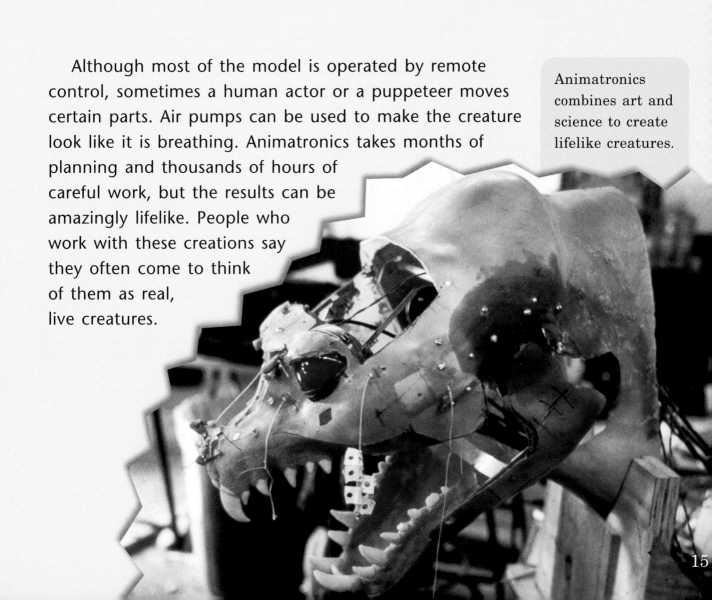

Although most of the model is operated by remote control, sometimes a human actor or a puppeteer moves certain parts. Air pumps can be used to make the creature look like it is breathing. Animatronics takes months of planning and thousands of hours of careful work, but the results can be amazingly lifelike. People who work with these creations say they often come to think of them as real, live creatures.

Animatronics combines art and science to create lifelike creatures.

But animatronics isn't the only way to create these special effects. Computer programs have been designed that allow moviemakers to build fantastic beasts. Special software is used to construct the creature's skeleton on the computer screen. That skeleton can then be programmed to make the creature perform whatever actions are called for in a scene. Once the movements are set, additional software is used to put muscles, bones, skin, and other elements on the creature, such as hair or scales.

Special computer software helps computer programmers design models of objects. Later details are added to make the objects look real.

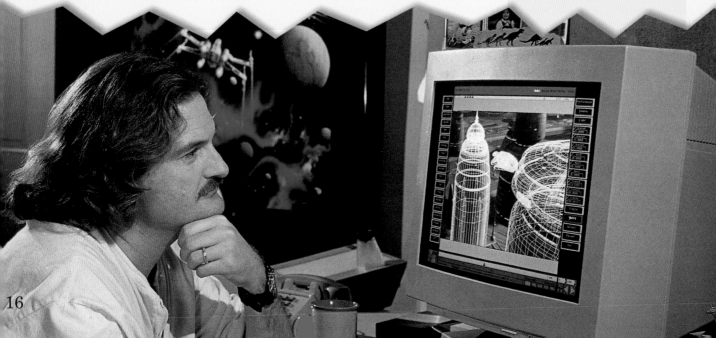

Computers can also be used to make real actors appear to grow hair, tails, horns, or whatever else the story calls for and to make real animals seem to talk. Sometimes computers save moviemakers money by creating crowds of people or strange beasts in the background of the main action. After all, which do you think is cheaper: hiring thousands of people to stand in a crowd, or copying the same 100 people over and over with a computer until they look like thousands of people?

5 Blue Screen Scenes

Some actors never travel to the location where the movie they're filming takes place. They may not even see the other people and things they are performing with in the movie. Instead, they perform entire scenes all by themselves in front of a big blue screen in a movie studio. Only later, when they watch the finished film, do they see themselves in the middle of a forest, perhaps fighting a giant spider!

Often moviemakers position film actors and models in front of a blue screen that is removed from the film later.

Blue screen is one of the most important special effects. It allows live actors to do things that seem impossible, such as flying, and it lets them act with characters made by computers. It can also put them in faraway places and worlds that exist only in the moviemaker's imagination.

Once the blue screen is replaced by a background of stars, this model ship looks like it is traveling across the galaxy.

How Blue Screen Works

If you've been to an action, fantasy, or science fiction movie, you've seen blue screen in action without even knowing it. Here's how it works.

1. First the actor is filmed in front of a brightly-lit blue screen.

2. Next the background that will eventually be in the scene is filmed or made by a computer separately.

3. Then the actor's blacked-out outline is combined with the shot of the background. Filming them together creates a black hole in the background.

4. After that the shot of the actor is combined with the blacked-out background.

5. Finally the shot of the actor is plugged into the empty hole in the background. Then they are filmed to make the finished scene.

21

6 Disaster!

Lots of trouble happens in movies: cars crash, ships sink, volcanoes erupt, and hurricanes rage. Many movie disasters are created by computers. Fantastic bolts of lightning, rivers of molten lava, fierce hurricanes, and terrifying tornadoes can all be safely created at a computer keyboard. Moviemakers then use blue screens to place actors in the scene.

But computers haven't taken over completely. Many disasters are filmed using other kinds of special effects. Among the most difficult and dangerous are those involving fires and explosions. Pyrotechnics experts (who specialize in these types of effects) must plan everything carefully to keep the actors and the movie crew safe.

Sometimes scale models are used, but other times real objects are blown up or burned. Fire and medical crews are always on hand in case emergency attention is needed. Since explosions and fires usually can be filmed only once, moviemakers use several cameras to make sure they film something that can be used.

Fire is difficult to fake. Even though images made by computers may be used to enhance a scene, real fire must be used as well.

Many movies have scenes that take place in the rain. Outdoors this effect is created using rain machines or hoses. Indoors actors perform in what looks like a giant shower. Water rains down from above, drains into a big pan, and is used again.

Lighting is important in filming a rain scene. If there's not enough light, the drops of water won't show up!

24

A storm at sea, which looks terrifying on screen, may be filmed in a water tank using scale model ships. Sometimes chemicals are added to make the water move more slowly. Then the model looks like a real ship riding the waves rather than a toy boat splashing around in a bathtub!

Some water scenes use water differently. To film a deep-sea movie, a dry set of the ocean floor may be built. Then the camera films through a clear glass tank filled with water to create the appearance that the scene took place under the sea!

After being filmed in a tank of water, this submarine model looks like it is traveling deep under the ocean!

Moviemakers can create blizzards and snowstorms, too. Outdoors snow machines (like those used on ski slopes) are put to work. But sometimes it may be easier and cheaper to film indoors.

Artificial snow, made from tiny flakes of plastic, can be blown through a wind machine to create the appearance of a blizzard. If plastic isn't available, moviemakers can use chopped-up feathers or even whitened cornflakes! The wind machine can be adjusted to blow the snow so that it gently falls down on an actor's shoulders or so that it strongly blasts against the actor's body. Some of these machines have engines powerful enough to run an airplane!

To make this scene seem wintry, special effects people were hired to blow snow on the trees and the ground.

To make snow on the ground, large salt crystals are used because they crunch underfoot just like real snow does. Plastic icicles dripping from roofs and actors bundled up in warm clothes complete the picture of a snowy, blowy scene!

This snowman may look real, but he is made entirely of fake snow. A real snowman would melt under the hot lights of a movie set!

27

Making a movie with special effects takes hard work and planning. It can be expensive, risky, and dangerous, too. Moviemakers are proud of the effects in their movies, but at the same time, they hope the effects won't really be noticed. They want moviegoers to be so caught up in the story that they don't stop to wonder, "How did they *do* that?"

Still, it's fun to go to a movie with special effects and try to figure out how they were created. Here are some scenes created with special effects.

Try to guess how each was done. Then turn the page to see if you were right.

Do you think a huge space shuttle was built for this scene?

How did the moviemakers create this giant ape?

Can you really ride across the galaxy in this ship? How was it captured flying on film?

29

Here's the story behind those special effects. How many did you figure out?

It costs a great deal of money to build a life-sized space shuttle. Instead, a model maker built a scale model of a space shuttle and surrounded it with tiny cars so it would look big.

The monster ape was a small model with a metal frame and a rabbit fur coat. Moviemakers combined a shot of the model with a shot of people in a theater so that the huge ape would tower above the crowd.

The spaceship below may look big on a movie screen, but it is actually just a small model! Thin, very strong rods help it hover in mid-air against a blue screen background. Then this shot is combined with a shot of deep space, and the spaceship looks like it is racing past the stars.

As moviemakers develop new technologies and try out new ideas, special effects get more exciting and incredible every year. Who knows what amazing things you might see on movie screens tomorrow? Whatever they are, maybe now you'll be able to figure out just how the moviemakers *did* that!

Index